Flight and *Pursuit*

Also by Dick Allen

Flight
and
Pursuit

Poems by

DICK ALLEN

LOUISIANA STATE UNIVERSITY PRESS

Baton Rouge and London   1987

Designer: Diane B. Didier
Typeface: Linotron Trump
Typesetter: G & S Typesetters, Inc.
Printer: Thomson-Shore, Inc.
Binder: John Dekker and Sons, Inc.

10 9 8 7 6 5 4 3 2 1

Library of Congress Cataloging-in-Publication Data

Allen, Dick, 1939–
   Flight and pursuit.

   I. Title.
PS3551.L3922F55   1987   811'.54   87-3242
ISBN 0-8071-1427-8
ISBN 0-8071-1428-6 (pbk.)

Grateful acknowledgment is given to the editors and publishers of the follow-
ing, in which some of these poems first appeared: *The Agni Review* ("The
Clergyman's Wife Composes a Spring Letter," "William Rimmer: *Flight and
Pursuit*"); *Connecticut River Review* ("Evening Train [1949]"); *Eleven* ("The
Perfect Mind"); *Michigan Quarterly Review* ("The Physicist to His Lost
Love"); *The North American Review* ("If You Visit Our Country"); *The On-
tario Review* ("Backstroking at Thrushwood Lake," "Clapping Erasers," "Cliff
Painting,"); *The Nassau Review* ("Night Driving"); *The New Criterion* ("The
Bookshop," "Cities & Empires"); *Poetry* ("Barge Lights on the Hudson," "The
Commuter," "Dignity," "Grandfather's Jigsaw Puzzle," "Notes After Ether,"
"The Poet at Eighteen"); *The Wittenberg Review* ("The Workers").

"Adirondack Town: An Idyll," "Crows and Windmills," and "The Postmaster"
first appeared in *The Hudson Review*. "Finale," "The Flutist," and "Lost
Love" were first published in *The New Yorker*.

"Sanibel Island" incorporates a number of phrases from Chapter 12 of *Roadless
Area*, by Paul Brooks.

My thanks to the National Endowment for the Arts and the Ingram Merrill
Foundation, for poetry fellowships which helped me to complete this book.

Publication of this book has been supported by a grant from the National
Endowment for the Arts in Washington, D.C., a federal agency.

for my parents: Richard Sanders Allen
Doris Bishop Allen

*—this fugue where you stand
at the start*

fugue . . . 1. A polyphonic musical style or form in which a theme or themes stated sequentially and in imitation are developed contrapuntally. 2. A pathological amnesiac condition during which the patient is apparently conscious of his actions but on return to normal has no recollection of them. . . . French *fugue,* or Italian *fuga,* flight, from Latin, flight.

—*The American Heritage Dictionary*

Contents

IV

I

"The unknown," said Faxe's soft voice in the forest, "the unforetold, the unproven, that is what life is based on. Ignorance is the ground of thought. Unproof is the ground of action. If it were proven that there is no God there would be no religion. No Handdara, no Yemesh, no hearthgods, nothing. But also if it were proven that there is a God, there would be no religion. . . . Tell me, Genry, what is known? What is sure, predictable, inevitable—the one certain thing you know concerning your future, and mine?"

"That we shall die."

"Yes. There's really only one question that can be answered, Genry, and we already know the answer. . . . The only thing that makes life possible is permanent, intolerable uncertainty: not knowing what comes next."

—Ursula K. Le Guin,
THE LEFT HAND OF DARKNESS

The secret is not to move, the lady said,
But sometimes you can turn your head away
For a minute, then back, as you do to really watch
A sunset, and you do this several times, and then
You can feel the dark on your eyes like a cold cloth.

That's how it was, she said. When the soldiers went by—
Straight lines of them, like holes in a cribbage board;
Men no older than my boy they caused to vanish—
I stood, but stared at nothing. Others told me
A haze of apple petals fell about them slowly.

And when I looked back, they were gone. The road
Was empty, save for cars with blackened seats,
And a body or two. It was comforting, that quiet,
For I was thinking of coffee, I was thinking
Of holding my hands around a cup of coffee.

You must do it, after all, she said—your eating,
Washing, sleeping, suffering. The mind has little rooms
It rents out to the body, and at times
You go there, no one follows you, the shades are drawn,
Dust falls like fingers from each one you touch.

NOTES AFTER ETHER

I'd wanted to bring back something from that darkness:
A spool, a few star flecks, a water lily . . .
But when I woke, I could remember only
The nurses' hands that held mine as I counted
Upwards and never reached ten, the doctor's face
Blurring into the ceiling as he disappeared.

Wheeled back to my room, I spent an hour watching
It rain into Bridgeport, how the rainfall kept
The streets, the porches of the tenements
Below my window deserted. I remember
A broken box kite dangling from a string
Caught on a power line . . . the O's of abandoned tires.

There had to be something. I closed my eyes and searched
Back into the darkness, as one does
When woken from dead sleep, looking for a cause
Of sweat on the temple, hands held stiffly outright,
Ready for a reencounter on whatever road
Went curving through the sycamores at midnight.

Yet, nothing. Under my left leg's bandages, the blood
Clotted, staining brown. The rental TV
Above my head, locked in its swivel assembly,
Offered the world through a simple set of knobs
I'd twist when I was ready. Now I was tired
And wanted none of it. My left leg throbbed,

My roommate lay drugged. Against the small window
Steadily rattling in its thin aluminum frame,
Cellophane rain gusts came and went and came,
Blurring and clearing and blurring the draggled city
Where Barnum once put elephants on show:
"If it doesn't play in Bridgeport, it won't play."

Then, one by one, my visitors pushed through the door:
Family, friends. In the softened crevices
Of their rain clothes, in their folded umbrellas
And finger-combed hair, scores of raindrops sparkled,
Catching fluorescent light. What more, what more
Had I ever wanted, should I have expected?

When they'd left, nurses' hands shooing them out,
A residue of books and rainy flowers
Lay scattered around my room. A bunch of doctors
From India came to inspect me—in their singing English
Pronouncing me salvaged, almost beyond doubt;
Smiled and nodded, and very shortly vanished.

My roommate gone, wheeled to his own operation,
I lay in the room alone. The rainfall slackened;
Houselights, streetlights, carlights—all that happened
To the world outside me patterning the glass
As Bridgeport fell away. I turned the television on.
I let the swarthy heroes have the darkness.

As you work with the faded pieces,
A man's head over here, the blue of the ocean
And sky still confused,
A huge elm growing by itself
Off in the corner,
You think of the world's old mistress, the moon
Looking in the window of a 19th-century poem,
And the summer patio
Where even the conversations about change
Don't change. You think of how many meanings
Drift into nothing, sure answers
Come to be disproved. Slowly, you form
A woman's body curving in a hammock,
The house in the distance,
And wonder why you seem about to weep
As the pieces get closer, bridges
Appear between the sections and dissolve
Into parts of the landscape;
And it is determined
That what you took to be a solid man
Was his broken reflection
Floating in a small pool by the garden's edge,
And the picture was something else
You had not dreamed of:
A landscape of a cottage by the sea
As evening was coming
So naturally it took you by surprise;
And the eastern barred owl
Nesting in the elm tree, fifty feet up,
Not minding how you worked your life away.

IF YOU VISIT OUR COUNTRY

At night, in the little towns that crop up in America
Where the highway curves beside a riverbank
Or lifts you suddenly up a drumlin to the lights
Left burning in closed restaurants and filling stations,
Someone is always walking with a dog, and someone
Is always standing at a window looking pensive.

And if you drive on further through the pensive
Fields and leaning forests of America,
Singing or dreaming, and you share the wheel with someone
You love, you will likely see a bank
Of stars in the west. Tune to an all-nite station
Playing crazy rock. The world will be blinking lights

Racing toward you or away, your headlights
Picking up old things along the highway: pensive
And dilapidated barns, abandoned railroad stations,
The culverts, junkyards, flagpoles of America
That never left the Thirties—the small-town bank
Closed for the Depression, then reopened. Someone

Is always starting out or starting over; someone
In jeans and open shirt has seen her name in lights
Or told a cowlicked boyfriend he can bank
Upon the future. In every town a pensive
Father reminisces to his son about America,
Or a priest is walking slowly through the Stations

Of the Cross, praying he might rise above his station
In this anguished life, becoming someone
Truly worthy, truly, truly worthy. All across America
You will find embracing lovers under streetlights,
Tiger lilies, Queen Anne's lace, the pensive
Look of high schools closed for summer, empty banks

Of bleacher seats at baseball games; and if you bank
Hard where the highway curves, and if you station
Yourself securely at the wheel, sooner or later pensive
Thoughts will overcome you. Try to be someone
For whom the country opens; for whom traffic lights
At empty crossroads signify America:

The shades and awnings of America, the kid who banks
A billiard shot, fizzed neon lights, the military station
High on Someone's Bluff, the sentry walking pensive.

WILLIAM RIMMER: FLIGHT AND PURSUIT

I saw two men in flight and in pursuit,
Stone castle walls around them and their bodies bent
As if they were the same. They were not the same
But in the leaning shadows of my dream
First I wore a dagger and a sash—
I fled the Lord's white lash;
Then a curving sword, a hood across my face—
I sped through darkness on His headlong chase.

I could not gain; I could not lose. We stayed
Near, not closing nearer. I could hear the wind
Roaring through the turrets, fleshing out the flags;
Beggars' hands reached up from beggars' rags,
Doorways turned to rooms; we sped through rooms
To other doorways—eyes, hands, bare thighs numb
As gods in bas-relief. The rooms went on and on;
Neither of us stumbled as we ran.

My mind, like all minds, sought a single room without
Another doorway; or, another world beyond it.
In either place I could have turned and drawn
My dagger from my sash; I could have shown
The face beneath this hood. But as we passed
Each portal, sandals burning, thinking it the last,
One more, one more. His sandals raced before
And followed me across each stone slab floor.

THE BOOKSHOP

You enter in the evening, after walking down
Three steps to a miniature courtyard and a door tied open
With a piece of brown twine. The table lamps
Have tassled shades the color of scorched parchment,
Tiny pools of yellowed light beneath them,
So that looking across the room seems like looking
Across a small autumn garden. The proprietor,
Wire-rimmed glasses glinting, nods but doesn't lift his head
From his reading and the rye bread sandwich
Into which he's nibbled an almost total moon.
You browse, and while you do, your hands
Grow heavy and old, as if by taking close-packed books
From their shelves you are pulling bricks from a wall
Bound to collapse should you remove too many
And not replace them. What you're searching for, among
These histories, these poems, these illuminated guides
To the soul, or the soul's companions . . . these compendiums
Of fossils, stars, speeches, journeys when the world
Was a path through forest or waves against painted eyes
On the bow of a wooden ship plying the Aegean,
Is a single line of calm. This evening, you come close,
Closer than ever before, for it starts raining
Outside among the streetlights, and a tabby cat
Does figure eights around your ankles, the proprietor
Sighs deeply behind you. When you turn, he's brushing
Specks of pale white brie and crumbs of bread
Carefully from the pages of his open manuscript
Into crumpled wax paper. Without a word
He takes the book you hand him, toting its price and tax
On the smudged back of an envelope, his stubby pencil
Writing small numbers. You pay him what he asks
And walk out into the rain, a black umbrella
Held high above you, the bookshop receding
Until it becomes a dab of flickering light
In the far reaches of Prague, or Budapest, or Rome,
Or what the eye sees when it looks down into
A heavily varnished painting found behind the stacks
Of books in a closet: dark city at night unknown,
Artist unknown, the light almost there, almost gone,
Rain and leaves and shadows on the cobblestones.

THE COMMUTER

On the Triborough Bridge, thinking of galaxies,
How Herschel said they strayed like garden beds
Seeding, blooming, fading, withering
Before his eyes as he stared back through Time,
I inch along in a cluster of April night
Traffic going home. Off to all sides,
The city's constellations: *Rachel's Dress,*
The Wineglass, The Cathedral Radio, Joe's Hat,
The Wad of Money, Whitman's Yawp, Crane's Leap
In storefront patterns and apartment lights.
Guarding the exit ramp, a girl with freckled hands
Holds yellow roses to each passing car.
I buy a dozen. Flung to the empty seat,
They toss and bend beside me down one spiral arm.

THE PHYSICIST TO HIS LOST LOVE

Last summer is months away and still the cicadas
Have not finished their stories. They keep telling them
As if they were responsible for every background
You keep stepping from. Some nights I dream we're standing
Under a streetlight, unable to touch;
Their familiar drone becomes so overwhelming
It almost seems we're sinking into their drab music
And soon will be only phosphors on a TV screen.

If worlds lie parallel, like rings around a barrel,
And if there is another me, another you close by
Or somewhere further back or further on,
Are we this intense, or less? How much
Can love diverge? In alternating worlds, do you still hold
Your hand up to your lips when frightened,
Pore over maps to find the hidden streams,
And read yourself to sleep with Henry James?

Or did you come from one of them, and have returned,
Leaving in your place a twin or clone
Who shares your memory but lacks the chromosome
Which held your disposition to be close to me?
"Der Herrgott würfelt nicht," and yet He may
With a sense of humor or despair. Immense beliefs
Topple from their own immensity;
We ride the waves to random eigenstates

As thought rides thought in search of certainty,
Or raindrops ride the branches of a withered tree.
Forgive. I'm so caught up in bubble chambers,
And studying the pathways of decaying particles
To check the probable, the language of the lab
Is a birth caul on the face of what I mean to say
About our love. Yet, I can't break free
To say it openly. Mock me if you must

But let my language try for its own dignity
However awkward is the merging of the scientific
With those splendid intuitions from your literature
By novelists and poets. Schrödinger's cat
May be living or sprawl dead. It may be the act
Of looking that decides. We have to look
And take our chances. All the universe I understand
Or seem to understand has been enraptured

With our observations. Last summer, when we walked
Across that meadow where the goldenrod

And Queen Anne's lace and black-eyed Susans poked
Every here and there above the swaying bunchgrass
You said our love was certain and would last,
But my mind turned upon itself and found no truth,
Although, God knows, I loved you. In my silence
Did the wave collapse or ripple when cicadas droned?

DIGNITY

Remington's almost oriental picture of the Indian
Seated on a horse and looking out
Across blue snowy plains to where the stars lie leveled
Like coals in a campfire doused in heavy snow
May express it: that single muted figure
Half wrapped in blanket and a long doomed ride ahead.
Who would not wish, or seem to wish
Such an ending for the human race: cold wind
And suffering accepted. In the posture
He is drawn in, and his frozen stature,
It's as if the world he lived through was entire;
He felt no shame, confusion, anguish
For being nameless in it, leaving no
Explanation of the snow squall, buried grass
And dreams of heavy bison and the hawk
Falling through the moonlight of a winter sky.
He probably was not much. But for a time,
There upon that ridge we can imagine, if we wish,
Not the pain to follow, not the horse gone lame,
The struggling cries of man and beast alone,
Their rotting bodies sprawled against a hillside,
But the tightening of muscle to be tried,
The lifted, blood-marred head,
And in that wish, our glory
Or delusion. Either brings us down
Who would imagine man is more than this
Brushed figure on a horse above the plains.

II

Emily came into view, her frowning face bent over a task. She wore a soft blue smock-like garment, like an old-fashioned child from a nursery, and she held a broom made of twigs, the kind used in gardens, and she was massing fallen leaves into heaps that were everywhere on the grass that floored this broken house. But as she swept, as she made her piles, the leaves gathered again around her feet. She swept faster, faster, her face scarlet, desperate. Her broom whirled in a cloud of yellow and orange leaves. She was trying to empty the house of leaves so that the wind could not spread them out again.

—Doris Lessing,
THE MEMOIRS OF A SURVIVOR

THE SWING

When I let go
   And way up there
Sat for a moment
   On thin air,

Feet dangling, hands
   Still shoulder-high,
I didn't hear
   Mother's cry

But only thought
   She'll love to see
Her offspring flying
   Crazily

Above her friends
   Across the yard;
I guess that's why she
   Pushed so hard.

THE POSTMASTER

A blue-haired woman in the house with trellises—
Beautiful big red roses like crushed drinking cups
Climbing up them toward the gingerbread—
Would rise every evening from her widow's bed
To greet my father. The mail he brought her
Wasn't much: a postcard from her niece, a flyer
From Montgomery Ward's, but he liked doing it,
He told me—it was something in his spirit,
That mysterious feeling that thrives on walking just
A step or two away from the beaten path
To do a favor. "Why not?" was always his answer
When someone questioned him about the other
People he befriended—like the Coshburns,
Our town's richest family, its only blacks, so spurned
By our neighbors, so envied, that I never
Remember anyone else out with us when we'd curve
Croquet balls on their great green lawn. There were also
The Hiroharas, he back from the camps. We'd go
Out bicycling and end up in their little garden
With the pool and small stone bridge and stunted pines
And pebble path, and boulders, flowers, and my father
Would have some tea. He would stir
It awkwardly, his hands too big. He looked funny
Nibbling sweet rice cakes. Everyone knew he was crazy
For those people, people who felt wrong the way he did
At the end of the 1940s when the maples spread
Over the oiled dirt roads, red roses grew
Higher and higher at the house of the blue-haired widow.

EVENING TRAIN (1949)

Where the D & H from Albany to Montreal
Curved in snowy woods beyond our town
We would kneel by creosote ties—and, bending down,
Place our ears to the rails.

Miles back, we could hear it: the 7:15
Cutting through pines, running on time,
Approaching the trestle high above Route 9
In a sound like wind makes in a small ravine.

And because we'd long practiced
Hearing the future, we knew when it slowed
At the D & H station, mailbags thrown to the road,
And then picked up speed—at the first

Straight stretch past the Lutheran church
Smashing into the woods. Even gripped tight,
Our hands couldn't feel it. Yet at the instant
Small bones in our ears began to lurch

We threw our bodies away, we rolled
Gasping and laughing down the steep embankment
Of weeds and snow and gravel and cement,
There to lie on our backs—and behold

The great beam of light. It split the pines,
It split our voices and it split our lives
Like they were nothing. The ties
Shook as it passed. Silent, we regained the lines

And balancing, balancing, foot after foot,
Tried to tightrope them home.
The loser was who fell off first. I remember the boom
Of ice on Jones' Pond: a boxcar door being shut.

NIGHT SLEDDING

From Lookout Hill it was a long way down to the village.
The plowed steep road no cars would dare until morning
And the pine trees snowed into each other, forming ruined
Castles and English manor houses and gamekeeper huts
In the ravines and gullies and stark on the ridges,
Seemed more ours than anything would ever be again,
Whether our lives were short or long. I glanced
At the others to see if they felt it: the loosened knot
Of boys whose fathers were mostly off in World War II,
Kneeling and panting in the snow, their bodies
Gnomed by bulky jackets, their faces small round windows
Sunk in wool, and saw their tremors
Of frozen-tongued awe, and how they tried to hide them
As I was trying, also, to not say anything
Too stupid or old. There were gusts of wind
Constantly sending clouds of powdered white
Off the rock outcroppings. Above us, a half-blasted moon
Was painted on a white sandpaper field of stars.

"Let's get going," someone said. Hand-me-down sleds
Lined up, lying on our bellies, boot tips dug into snowruts,
We studied the village below us, the far-off lights
Of the D & H station, the Methodist church steeple,
Lights in the upstairs windows of a dozen cottages
And "Isn't this something," the boy beside me whispered,
"Isn't this something!" Who started, I don't remember,
But suddenly, faces held up, yelling for dear life,
All of us yelling and whooping, we were steering
Our sleds in great S's as we fell,
None of us trying to win, all of us half-crazed, shouting,
"Watch out! Hang on! Steer to the side!
Steer to the middle! Drop behind! Go ahead!"
Sparks from rocks our runners scraped, and then
At the last sweet drop, an absolute silence among us
As we swooped down, and some of our mothers and sisters
Waiting beneath the streetlights, some applauding
With soft mittened claps as we slowed. Walking home,
My house the last one before the village became a meadow,
I saw a comet streak, leaving in its wake
A crowfoot of light, gone the moment I blinked.

Five times, the men dived through ice. At last
They pulled out his body
From the channel between Round Lake and Little Lake
That winter I was eleven
And snow lay over our tiny Methodist village
Like a webbing of white fishing nets, each house
A colored float. I remember, days later,
Walking by myself among broken cattails
To where I could stand looking out upon that place
Thin ice gave in, he clung to its breaking edges
For as long as he could, his best friend running
Away through falling snow. Now, nothing was left there
But a trample of footprints, a few sled tracks,
And a hole frozen over. Above me, two crows
Cawed their way across a bright blue sky.
I tried to remember what I could about Junior Marcuchi
But all that came back was a summer afternoon he'd ridden
His bike with playing cards clothes-pinned to its spokes
And stopped by the water fountain where I played
To take a drink and splash his face. . . . I turned
From the way I'd come, following some old
Boot-holes into the marsh, feeling sun on my face
Until I reached two rusty streaks of iron: the D & H
Railroad line that led off to far hills
Through the beautiful woods and world and trunks of oaks
I splattered with snowballs, testing my pitching arm.

CLAPPING ERASERS

Numbers and words go up in blue-white puffs
At the ends of my hands. Here, on the school's back porch,
I make the erasers do a Morse code SOS
Until, like minds at Recess, each is cleansed.

I can see Round Lake from here, and Lavery's pontoon planes;
One is revving up, about to take
The fast run toward the pines. It will almost skim them
On its way to Saratoga or Mechanicville.

At twelve, I'm caught in Time and loving it:
The unmown grass, the marble ring, the Ford
With running boards my father lets me stand on,
And my teachers, Mrs. Copins and Miss Turner

Who (and Lavery) will die throughout the Sixties.
But now they pass out Coca-Cola rulers
And teach us Tennyson and Browning, and despite ourselves
Machine-gun recitation of times tables.

I even have a paper route. Each morning
On my Shelby bike, I pedal through my village
And throw the news through railings, or tuck it inside doors.
It's all about the halves of Jell-O boxes,

Truman, and MacArthur, and the Brooklyn Dodgers.
It's all about my life, but I don't know that yet.
Another city of another place on earth
Vanishes each time I clap erasers.

And one of Lavery's planes is coming down,
Circling, and then it hits the waves.
Its pontoons leave a wash like puffy railroad tracks
Into the lily pads where Mr. Lavery stands,

Flagging the pilot in. My arms are white and scratchy;
My face looks like a mime's. One more call for help
Before I'm done. When Miss Turner leans
Out of her window, I'll be her boy of dust.

CROWS AND WINDMILLS

Crows and windmills—sounds of American farmland
When the sky is overcast and the wind blows at evening,

As someone like Burchfield would know, taking down his easel
In the Depression, and starting the long stroll back

Through a meadow of swaying bunchgrass to the county road
Where his running-board Ford is waiting tiredly

Pulled to the side, and gray as weathered clapboard
Of houses that seem to exist only in distance.

Tonight, I heard them again, but it was in a movie
And only for some minutes while a girl in overalls

Walked with her head down from her drunken father
Toward a hill and a tree like a clawed hand toppling over

Against the October sky. I shivered. The windmill's blades
Blurred in a wooden cluttering; the crows made dives

Toward the open silo, cawing and cawing with that
Raw scratch of the throat that makes me think *O Sinner-Man,*

Where you gonna run to! Such heavy loneliness
Came over me I had to grip the next row's empty seatback

Until the scene was done. I had been returned
To Roark's farm, and had heard a third sound: the dry

Snap and whisper of thousands of rows of cornstalks
A gang of us were playing in, losing ourselves on purpose,

Then leaping high as we could to see above them, calling
Our names out: A parody of what would become our lives,

Moon bleeding, stars falling, sea sinking, rocks rolling
All on that day. As a joke, my friends snuck off, and I

Was left leaping and calling to no one when the dusk
Came on. Desperate, I leaped and called and leaped and called

Among the cornstalks until, exhausted, I fell
And rolled over, panting; in the overcast, I saw

A flock of crows, the pattern so jagged it was almost vicious.
Each crow, as the flock passed above me, cawed out its warning

More to itself than others; and when, at last, I followed
The windmill sound, it became a huge gray daisy

Whirring above the barn. . . . Farmer Roark found me
And drove me home in a red truck splattered with rust

When I couldn't stop crying and shaking. My parents
Had not known I was gone, worked to the bone as they were.

THE WORKERS

They make their way up the hill in Burchfield's painting
So tiredly, so one by one, it is as if their bodies
Are still at the lathes. My father, like this, came home
Winters from the railway yards. Often he didn't talk
For hours as my brother and I played around him,
Climbing his belly, pretending he was dead
While he lay on the big flowered couch and watched our mother
Stand at her ironing board in the kitchen doorway
Or pass back and forth before him, hands in an apron
She even wore, sometimes, over her nightgown.

II

In another Burchfield painting, at six o'clock
I wait in a snowdrift near a row of houses
While my family has supper. Great long icicles
Hang from gray eaves and porches. The backdoor steps
Are shoveled only enough for a single person
To climb without slipping. Through curtainless windows
I see bare walls above the heads about the table,
Except for a shelf that holds the plain white pitcher
And bowl I will one day break. Two houses down,
Floating beyond a chimney and just barely there,
A sideways crescent moon. I tell you this
So you might come to the streets of Steubenville,
Springfield, and Detroit, and Gary, Indiana.

THE POET AT EIGHTEEN

In the cab of a truck bound straight across Ohio,
    To earn my ride
And keep the driver sharp against the traffic flow
    One night I tried

Right out of my freshman textbooks to convince
    Him of all things
To know thyself was best, and since
    To that iron string

Each heart beats true, each man should undergo
    The search within
Or with his dying gurgle will not know
    That he has been

Alive. The driver was amused, and stayed awake
    But said he'd heard
Those thoughts before. His large foot worked the brake
    To miss a furred

Thing stumbling from the bushes. In the greenish light
    I saw him pop
A benny, swallow it with spit, then sight
    The first snowdrop

Upon our windshield, rub it out. "Damn," he said,
    "It means we'll reach
Indiana like we're on a goddamn sled."
    He said that each

Five miles slower was another half an hour
    From town to town—
More minutes when he could not sleep, or wear
    A woman down.

It was a mighty snowstorm. At its end
    He slid the truck
Beside a clapboard house, and left me there, went in
    To try his luck.

A soft loose woman's shadow met the curtains,
    Then retreated.
I looked away. A stone deer sniffed the lawn
    For crusts of bread.

Freezing, wrapped in blankets, I began
    To draw my face
Upon the frosted mirror. It took me until then
    To know my place.

VETERANS DAY

You were the soldier shouting at the rain
Who walked the college campus with a puzzled look,
Brought back, without parade, from Vietnam.

Once I hated you, your uniform, your name,
The way you hunched with buddies in an open truck.
You were the soldier shouting at the rain.

I was the marcher with a cause to claim,
Jailed so many times I thought I'd crack.
We wanted no more deaths in Vietnam.

But the helicopter war went on . . . and on—
A country ravaged when green locusts struck;
You could hear them coming through the rain.

A child could kill you, or a crippled man.
You trusted nothing; you got high for luck
And stared through burning eyes at Vietnam.

I burned my draftcard with a lighter flame.
I marched on Washington. You marched the jungle muck.
Necessity? Or madness. *Who can stop the rain?*
We were young men in the days of Vietnam.

III

Seek transfiguration. Deliver the wet shining soul. For Death will make a story of you. It will say you have done the right thing. That you've added to the stock of blessed beings and made a modest run. Oh Love, I don't like the word on me, this drift through the blood of my obsolescence. That my biological time is over. That I've used up the world.

—E. L. Doctorow,
"LIVES OF THE POETS"

NIGHT DRIVING

Cold hands on the cold wheel of his car,
Driving from Bridgeport, he watches
The long line of red taillights
Curving before him, remembers
How his father used to say they were cats' eyes
Staring back at them, a long line of cats
Watching from the distance—never Fords,
Buicks, Chevrolets, filled with the heads
Of children, lovers, lonely businessmen,
But cats in the darkness. Half asleep,
He can believe, or make himself believe
The truth of his father—all the lies
Not really lies: images which make
The world come closer, cats' eyes up ahead.

ADIRONDACK TOWN: AN IDYLL

Mountain interference kills the radio
And I am home again.
White pines cling to the upper Sacandaga
As if they were holding it from closing: nurses' hands
And the wound runs deep and old. The cold
Wind from Canada is blowing wooden rowboats
Against their wooden docks, clunking and splashing,
And every puddle in the road this evening
Has a little lattice of ice that's crept across it,
I break as I walk. It's not as if
Time stood still—the ESSO sign at the corner
Is EXXON, and the cemetery gate is padlocked—
But that it eddies here, as thought sometimes
Will meet with stiff resistance and curve off,
Leaving a deeper pool beneath a bluff of shale,
One you can swim across with several strokes,
Or dive and touch bottom—something I have missed
Ever since childhood. Not strangely, my impulse
Is to whistle, and I do: "Vaya Con Dios,"
"A Man in a Raincoat," "The Great Pretender,"
But stop when a porch door opens and a girl comes out,
Takes one look at me and disappears,
Her face a weeping petal in a woolen cowl. Fog swirls
On the peaks of Hadley, Marcy, and I think of comets—
Their tails like rivers shorn from their beginnings—
As they go parabolic through the universe. A collie,
In a backyard with a clothesline, barks a tired
Warning, then just growls. A few thin snowflakes
Fall beneath the town's one streetlight marking
Where the road turns up toward Conklingville
And I turn back. This winter will be a rough one:
Rock-holes in the Old Mill windowpanes
Mean more joblessness. Kerosene lanterns. The smell
Of woodsmoke and new cords of wood stacked where
There used to be lawns. And now a boy
Appears behind me on a bicycle,
Slows to give me wide berth, pedals on
Until he goes, no hands, into his driveway.
At the bridge
Where I've parked my battered car beside the stone
Abutment carved with Uncle Rollin's name, I lean
Over the parapet. Floating upon the water,
The moon is a bicentennial medallion; even stars

Seem to be floating, though they might be lily pads
Spangled by distance. My hands are clenched
Into themselves. Oh my God,
And what if this should end? The Sacandaga
Spills from the Adirondacks like dark blood
Of wolf and deer and of the great bear roaming.

ON THE WAY

Someone had left a copy of the *Tao*,
A vase of cattails, and a writing pad
On the old motel dresser. Outside my room,
The traffic on Route 1 was constant
Far into the night. I wrote
To a full moon pale in the curtains
And a distant, barking dog. The next day
It rained as I drove. "Windex clean"
My parents would have called this morning,
Crows and seagulls in the air along the coast,
My destination *Weeping Gray*—your house
High as a hermit's cabin among the boulders.
You waited on the tiny lawn out back,
The painting before you only one stroke done,
Yet already in it, five tall misty flowers
Beside the empty pool and rainy path.

ROCKPORT, MASSACHUSETTS

I stand with my uncle.
Unlike Eliot, he calls these three rock islands
Lying offshore
(As in "to save from loss or destruction")
The Salvages.

He's in his eighties, a doctor.
Recently he reread all of Darwin's journals.
The more his memory goes, the more he reads,
"Trying to stuff the holes with knowledge."
He courted and married my aunt when she was sixty-five.

Accepting his binoculars, I watch
How the waves smash up against the islands' sides,
Sending a carpet of foam that turns transparent
Onto them. "I've never seen," I say,
"Anything so desolate, so hopeless."

He nods, and I can't tell if he heard me.
"Yes, they're beautiful," he says.
Sometimes at night, he dreams
A trading schooner's come apart upon them,
And in his dream he rescues skeletons.

"Jesu hath merci" reads a stone
In the Rockport Cemetery where his people lie:
Relatives and patients, one of whom he cured
Of fifteen separate illnesses before she died
Hale and hearty in an auto crash.

His strong, gaunt body
Leads me through the rocks. "I can get quite far
Into stories but I can't remember ends. Sometimes," he says,
"It's just as well." I slip. He doesn't. Down the hill
We find a beach of perfect rounded stones.

Most are bird-egg sized. "The sea did that to them,
Rolled them and rolled them, like people—
People who go nowhere and do nothing,"
He observes. Even to the highest house, the roar
Of ocean covers Rockport in gray leaves.

LOST LOVE

You're in the City, somewhere. I suppose if I stood
On Times Square a year or two I'd find you,
Face pleasant and older, coming out of the subway crowd,
Or studying poinsettias in a florist's window.
A flicker—that would be all. Both of us
Looked so much like others, which of us could be sure
We were not others? Once, we met in a glance.
So too, in a glance, should both of us disappear.

But I'm lying. Often on West Coast or East,
I'll be at a movie before the lights go down
And Beauty flees through the meadows from the Beast
Or the boy steps out of a throng to claim his crown
When far down the aisles and rows I'll see you there,
Your body still young, your eyes, your taffeta hair!

POEM FOR MY 44TH BIRTHDAY

I

More than midway through, I wake this morning
To the doctor's violin. He plays a Mozart sonata
And it's like a trembling wineglass spilling from its brim.
I lie a long while in bed, my thoughts
Upon Planck's Time, the splintered instant from which all life came
After that speck of space changed into matter, flung
Forth the universe. High on one wall
A sepia print in which a nude lies sprawled
Upon a Chinese robe. She, too, is composed, a physicist might say,
Of the matter of the stars, as all of us, all things
(The poplar leaf half-green, half-rot that sways
Outside my bedroom window) are composed. Then the music halts,
Leaving a little lap of silence in the air
Before the cicadas, a cardinal's two-note song,
The cars on the Merritt Parkway fill it in.

II

Late in the afternoon, my presents opened,
I backstroke Thrushwood Lake, watching for the muskrat
That lies in Boehmke's Cove. Twice each day
But not on schedule, he swims its length and back,
Leaving in his wake two intersecting V's.
The sky's the shade of blue that's almost white
(A Wedgewood color) and the twenty swaying willows
Seem great heads of hair from Merlin's world
Broken into ours. Turning, I remember
My daughter's love affair with miracles—how all
One afternoon when she was five she kept
Pointing at a rock, a tree, a flower, shouting
"Miracle! A miracle! A miracle!" until it sounded like
"America!" Walking the short way home,
I toss a pebble high into the air and catch it.

III

After the evening television and the evening love,
I push the screen door open. It's a country night
Of lawn-chair shadows and the waning moon. Up in the field
Wings of bats and moths move silently
Like fragile waves of light and matter floating
Through all substances, or speckled images on photographic plates
Astronomers hold up: novas, quasars, pulsars flickered back in time.
If physicists are right, if I am not defined
By my form of body or my frame of mind
Am I set free to recognize and praise (the lovely obscure ways)

When consciousness aligns with harmonies? From next door
Mozart once again, this time on record, brief and dying,
And every house along my tiny street lies dark.
Down from the lake, a splash. Muskrat? Probably not.
Only a willow branch has fallen to the waters.

THE FLUTIST

My dreamy cousin, I see you standing on a ledge
Above the Batten Kill.
You seem to be waiting for someone,
Head to the side, your tall body all alert—

Even at sixteen
Already waiting, as if you already knew
The many small apartments, many small jobs
You would never quite want,

The men not quite loyal, the music
You love so much
Never quite perfected,
But blown from your lips the best that you knew how,

And your life, like most of ours,
A series of small recitals and arpeggios
Before a few
Ladies in folding chairs—

Waiting for someone, waiting
Almost on tiptoe
Upon a ledge, among the pines,
Above the Batten Kill.

CANADA

Nineteen years ago, one night we smoothed
A map of Canada down on your dorm-room table
And said the names out loud: Prince Edward Island,
Saskatchewan, Quebec, and Manitoba.
Someday we'd roam them in an old junk car
At speeds from twenty to spectacular,
Hell-bending lives out for the jugular.

You pranced around the table, saying Eskimo,
Sioux Lookout, Hudson Bay, Blind River, Hearst.
Posed dramatically beside the open window,
In your great voice you read us Robert Service.
I'd write a book. You'd write a book. They'd be
Fired with adventure, smoked with mystery,
Aurora borealis of our century.

Just think of it, you said. Our hearts will break.
We'll camp beneath the pines of Yellow Knife,
And walk out on the ice of Great Slave Lake,
Canada our blessing, Canada our life.
How strange to us the streets of Edmonton,
Swift Current, Maple Creek, and Saskatoon.
To hear the wolves in concert with the loon!

Armstrong Station, Tiptop Mountain, Cape St. John—
We'd reconnoiter all. You grew
So excited that you flung your glasses down
And hugged yourself like Lowell used to do.
Outside your doorway other undergraduates
Whose learning came in lesser starts and fits
Were drunk on drink, and seemed our opposites.

Why tell the rest? Of course we didn't go.
A dream is one thing and a task another.
The first hits tree trunks and the latter snow,
And when they separate they leave a blur
Like wet fog on the roads of Valleyview,
Your life and mine, high passes broken through,
Or like the sea smoke rising out of Baie Cameau.

IV

*I had just discovered what it means to see the world through an-
other man's eyes. It is a discovery you are lucky to make at any age,
and one that is no less marvelous whether you make it at fifty or
fifteen. Because it is only then that the world, as you have seen it
through your own eyes, will begin to tell you things about yourself.*
—Peter Taylor,
"PROMISE OF RAIN"

CLIFF PAINTING

The girls who asked you to do it were the kind who leaned
Against you and no more. I don't think they knew the danger
Up there, at dawn when the cops wouldn't spot you.

I know I was scared. But I was also in love,
So deeply in love my hair would stand on end
Whenever I thought of her. That's why, one morning,

Brush and a can of paint in my old Boy Scout knapsack,
I started to climb. I was so crazy, I'd planned
To paint the biggest heart ever, and fill it with our names,

So the whole valley could see it, and every driver
On the Interstate—maybe even someone looking down
From a low-flying plane. . . . At first it was easy

As I passed the names of junior high school kids,
A few peace signs, a "Black is Beautiful," a "Stop the War,"
Several Bob Dylans and three Rolling Stones—

No pun intended. But then I began to come upon
The highest names, the ones from boys in college
On athletic scholarships, names of the weirdos

Who'd dare anything, and I realized I hadn't thought
This whole thing out enough. Every accessible place
Was taken with a name or heart, or both, and I knew

They must have used ropes, teams of boys with ropes
Had climbed before me, swinging out into space
To declare their love, allegiance, or obsession

At some risk of death. . . . I clung for a long time up there,
Looking down at the valley, thinking of my love, and hearing
What she would say if I failed. It started to drizzle

And a few small pebbles tumbled from the crevice
Where I was wedged. Pieces of moss came loose.
The valley darkened slightly. I closed my eyes and imagined

Falling, and my girl and parents at my funeral,
Then who she would marry instead. . . . And yet, you know,
I wanted fame and immortality right then—so if

Later I failed, wherever I was I could think of someone
Looking up at the cliff and seeing what I'd done, and maybe
For a moment I'd be someone other than a man

With a beer belly, sitting at a bar like this and reminiscing
Over what? Over love, that's what. I kept on climbing
And I found a place, I almost killed myself, but should

You look up now you'll see us, though the letters
Are somewhat faded and the heart looks like a kidney,
And later someone wrote above me even larger.

Still, I didn't marry her. At the end, we really fought
One night at the revival drive-in, Dean and Wood and Mineo
Together in the dark. She even wanted me

To climb again, to paint us over, and I laughed.
No way, I told her. Often I think of her trundling with her kids
And husband through the valley, and she glances

Up and there she is, with me again, forever
Linked with me upon the mountainside. . . . I'm glad I did it.
That's love for you. And also, that's revenge.

His bad eye, the one that's losing vision,
Blurs, and much of the right side of his life
Becomes outline and vapor.
He's learning that he must turn consciously,
As toward a still life with a skull—the grapes
Overly ripe, shadows and moisture upon them,
And in those tiny caves where light has entered.

This evening, lurching to avoid the lights
Of a quickly approaching car, he stepped too far
Into wet blossoms of a fully blooming dogwood:
Incredible softness veined by deeper branches,
The momentary glowing as he groped for balance.
Reaching to catch him,
I saw the dried blood ending each white petal.

War was on TV when we returned, a blurry war
Waged by distant instruments and outright turnings,
And our children sat watching, their frozen bodies
Strewn upon the couch, the chairs, the rug.
It isn't pretty. It isn't the way I would have it,
But something is leaving us—the foliage behind it
Closing, as after a horseman riding through deep forest.

He's fine when it's dark and the room is very familiar,
Clock to the left of the dresser.
Our radio is playing us some Ives or Copland,
And he talks about the skyline of a county carnival,
A lighted ferris wheel revolving at its apex.
Love, he says, must have some swaying to it,
Some elevation and some desperateness.

Yet if only he could see whole! More and more often
He jerks his head sideways,
Sensing at his elbow what is nowhere near
Or only the padding of the cat across the floor.
His constant wandering is growing stronger,
As if he's finally understanding how we all
Must fumble in the grapevines for the skull.

Brave, blurry man. I love it when he touches
My face in the dark and asks me if I've seen
Angels or devils. I roll against him,
Not much to do, I know, but it is better
Than cursing or crying, punished past belief.
The irises came up, I meant to tell you,
And the heal-all on our lawn is one vast city.

Two Poems

THE PERFECT MIND

Each stone of the garden
Carefully set
After days of thought

So that anywhere
A leaf might fall
Will be correct.

WINTER RONDEAU

Maybe an owl returning to the forest
Sees, in the distance, one light in our house
And you standing there, your naked breasts
Offered to moonlight, and your peasant blouse
Slipped down your shoulders as you look toward the forest
Where all the night things go, or seem to go,
And hunger and passion sleep, and all
Is tremolo and cameo—
                    maybe an owl.

Momentary beds of white burst flowers
    Appear behind us. Kicking and pulling,
We continually create what disappears,
    So keep from drowning.
And what a sky is overhead! Great medieval blurs
    Of cumulus ascending.

We reenact da Vinci's naked man
    With four arms, four legs, fingertips
And feet in square and circle to explain
    Proportion. Or imagine hips
Rocking in a snowfield: we have lain
    Down in snow, and left snow angel trails

From one side to the other, or a vertical
    String of paper dolls, joined head to toe across
Still waters. If we yell
    Out for the joy of it, or toss
Our heads from side to side, this spell
    Is exultation, just as it is madness.

Our elemental madness—that we know we live
    Today, this century, this year, this hour, minute
Everything is happening. Above,
    A flock of geese goes flying down towards Bridgeport.
Emerging in a high and cloudy cave,
    A Boeing's shadow is a crosslike print

To which you raise your head. The shore
    Is sand and willows—and our children
Floating near it, bobbing heads and figures
    Flattened on their plastic rafts. The wind
Blows them toward each other;
    Or away, unless they link their hands

While we tread water. Look at them. Their moments
    Also disappear, yet last—the paradox
Of memory. Think of mullein weeds,
    Full and empty pods upon their stalks,
Dead flowers and the living seeds,
    The washcloth texture of their flannel leaves,

And turn around. Stay close to me. Leave froth
    Again behind us and to both our sides.
Nothing ever will be beautiful enough
    Unless we're satisfied with how we ride
Waves backward and can love,
    For what we fashion, though we cannot keep, we need—   47

As I, these living moments, need the lake against
    My back, those towers in the clouds, the cries
Of children linking hands, the houses fenced
    About the lake, their windows brimmed with sky
Blue and white—trapped in the way your glance
    Catches me, and holds me, and all meanings fly.

BARGE LIGHTS ON THE HUDSON

for Dana and Mary Gioia

Glass door to the balcony slid open,
We step from the party to a night so clear
Only diamonds could scratch it. Below us,
River barges look like floating dominoes,
And we seem to hear boatmen singing, but that may
Be simply chanteys from another condominium
Along these cliffs. Hours, you say,
Should pass as slowly and as beautifully
As those lights on the Hudson. Leaning here
Against the railing, shoulders barely touching,
We play a child's game of connect-the-dots
To bring out of the dark a tiny tugboat
In which a phantom pilot, legs spread wide apart,
Wholeheartedly steers—his face
Rimose as the moon's. One by one,
Others join us, until all along
The balcony a line of men and women
Lean and whisper, staring down, and some
Say the river's asphalt, others that
U-galaxies drift there,
Or we are in a science-fiction movie
Watching starships in a planet exodus
Across the Coalsack. Soon, however,
The party flares up in the living room, those few
Who linger here grow silent, watching until all
Lights disappear toward Troy, and just the oars
Of Irving's ghost row out from Tarrytown.

Although the clematis are out, it's still a somber morning
As we wait for our son. He should be crossing Pennsylvania now
In the dawn, the Greyhound bus tires steaming
Against the wet highway, and the residue
Of last tests still in his head. Perhaps he's just caught sight
Of a John Deere tractor climbing up a hill
Or one of those gray-wood houses you expect
To see in the distance when the mind's half full
Of sleep and thought. Or, head against his wadded sweater,
He's thinking of some girl. Or waterfall. I turn from the window
Where forty-four—I've counted—blossoms have appeared
Among the leaves that climb our trellised patio,
And try to be with him, remember everything
I can: voices over cards, the slight jouncing of a suitcase
In the overhead rack, tensed or untensed faces, the fling
Of bodies forward when the driver brakes in haste,
And boredom (boredom stays the same),
The towns, the villages brief flashings-by,
Birthdates, deathdates, lines and scenes and names,
All the facts and figures I once easily supplied
Fading into butter, buttercups, the rhododendron
And clematis by the porch, my parents on the lawn
They've left for me to cut. Not soon enough, but soon,
Philadelphia, and Newark, and New York, and home.

SANIBEL ISLAND

Deep in our forties, we follow the jagged line of sea wrack
For miles in the early morning sun.

Far to the south, a melted checkerboard pattern
Of black and white willets slides up and down the sky

And nearer to us, cormorants have perched motionless
On old channel markers. Pant legs rolled,

We search for the promised shells: tiny, bright coquinas,
Each the size of a small child's fingernail;

Sundials, lightning whelks; in the folds of seaweed,
Angel wings, junonia, the staircase at Blois

Miniaturized in a conch's inner spirals,
The fallen gas station emblem of a lion's paw.

All this cast-up wealth! It is as if we are strangers
Sent to some storm-washed city on a mission

More sacred than we've been told, and among thousands
Of broken, wave-worn, and eroded faces

Must find beauty and calm. A flock of white ibis
Struggles into the mangroves; snowy egrets,

The bold black brushstrokes of their bills and legs
Like Japanese paintings come to life,

Settle beside them. Osprey and zebra butterflies
Seem everywhere. Bending to lift a moon shell,

I notice a mollusk quickly drawing in its siphon,
The tiny squirt of water before it disappears

Below the wet sand. A plover suddenly gives
Its sad three-note whistle; on the surface of a tidal pool

The knobs of a sunken alligator's eyes emerge,
Then sink again. And when I stand

You are pointing out to sea. The black skimmer,
Creasing the water with his down-turned beak,

Is headed straight toward us. Only at the last
Minute does he turn and veer across the mudflats

As silently as he came. The coot are muttering;
A pair of boat-tailed grackles noisily builds a nest

In the sun-splashed hummock behind us—where we'll rest
Before our slow walk back among the scattered shells.

FINALE

The music was thrilling. But when we left the concert
Gullies of rain washed down between those buildings
Lining the dark street up to the subway station,
And pockmarked your naked shoulders as we walked
Slowly, resigned. For a moment, I thought
Of doing a bright Gene Kelly on the pavement,
But you looked so drowned, so unhappy
I bullied slightly ahead—the rainstorm too loud
Even for yelling. There is a tiny passage
In *Tender Is the Night* where the hero, Dick Diver,
Knows everything's over. Everything. And it's so simple:
A brief streak of sky, a storefront boarded up,
Strands of wet hair plastering our skulls,
A thousand rainy windows to Far Rockaway.